REAL CUTE DANGER

Angela Cleland was born in Inverness in 1977. She studied at the University of Glasgow and Goldsmiths College. Cleland writes poetry, science fiction and fantasy. She's had a variety of jobs to fund her writing habit, including store detective, knowledge engineer, business analyst, e-learning professional, poetry tutor and audiobook narrator.

ISBN: 978-1-915079-86-2

Cover designed by Aaron Kent & Emma Kennedy

Edited & Typeset by Aaron Kent

Broken Sleep Books Ltd
Rhydwen
Talgarreg
Ceredigion
SA44 4HB

Broken Sleep Books Ltd
Fair View
St Georges Road
Cornwall
PL26 7YH

Contents

Real Cute Danger

Angela Cleland

for Jacob and Cammy

SCENE ONE

INT. SUBURBAN HOUSE/DOWNSTAIRS

The lights are variously on and off. Enter, EXPECTANT MOTHER, holding a pregnancy test. She is envisioning things enclosed within other things – conkers, Russian dolls, Ferrero Rocher, bullets in their chambers, all leguminous vegetables. For the first time, she is a layer, a Kinder-egg capsule, a pass-the-parcel – ask at your peril how she feels about onions. UNWITTING FATHER sits playing Football Manager 2010.

                    EXPECTANT MOTHER
                    (takes a breath)
                                        CUT TO:

At two weeks past conception

you are already building your eyes – I panic –
what do I know about eyes? The picture
is upside-down when it hits your retina;
women see better in the dark than men;
a flash of their whites is as good as a rabbit's tail
to send us scampering for our burrows.

But to build one, never mind a pair, from –
what have you got? I don't even know
the ingredients – proteins? amino acids?
I place a hand on my belly and focus
on your behalf. At each division
we could flunk this: I'm back at school.

All I can do is slide you my jotter
and whisper – *I have eyes – copy mine.*

Spoiler

I laugh at the bicycle, chained to the railings at this forgotten station. It's spray-painted yellow. And I mean YELLOW – custard 'n' mustard served up in a banana skin, on a beach, to a cartoon lion. And I mean *spray-painted* – the frame, the handlebars, the handlebar grips, the reflectors, the pedals, the wheels, presumably anything that was behind it when it was sprayed. All that has resisted is the pink plastic baby-doll seat, and some lucky scraps of tyre. You say, 'Hang on,' and take out your phone.

I'm still giggling as the train pulls away, but as I snap a photo, the joke turns to nightmare, a clown's face running in the rain – tears of paint are still drying on the frame. Smear one off on your finger, lick it. It would taste of desperation, of the sweat of a father, the father of a child with a wish – an eyes-screwed-tight, fingers crossed wish for a yellow bike – a father who, days before the wish was wished, spent his last on a pink bike with a baby-doll seat on the last day of the closing down sale of the only bike shop for forty miles. A father drunk on need and maybe on something harder, who sobs as he tosses the spray-can and wipes his yellow-as-a-cur hands on his jeans. Who sobs again as he chains the bike to the railings, a warning to all would-be WORLD's BEST DADs, before he staggers out onto the tracks.

The light from your phone – you are scrolling, peeling away my daydream. You say, 'Knew it – it's to do with the Tour de Yorkshire. They're everywhere.' And I believe it must be true, that last bit.

The Developing Soul

Studies show that eating too many nuts
is bad for the baby.
Studies show that not eating enough
nuts is bad for the baby.

Your baby is now the size of a lentil.

Always sleep on your left-hand side
to increase the flow of good dreams to the baby.
Always sleep facing an open window.
Never start a vendetta with a fox.

Your baby is now the size of a conker.

Avoid negativity. War, climate change,
and all manmade and natural disasters
are bad for the baby. But be compassionate –
an indifferent existence is bad for the baby.

Your baby is now the size of a kumquat.

Do not take paracetamol unless
the impact on the baby of your personal suffering
is likely to be worse for the baby
than the baby having a moderately raised
likelihood of developing asthma.
Negative emotions affect the baby.
Don't let your pain lead to negativity.

Your baby is now the size of a clown's fist.

Wonder is everywhere. Let it seep into you.
This is good for the baby. The baby
feels when you are overawed.
Make everything beautiful, see the good
in everything. But don't overdo it.
Hyperventilation is bad for the baby.

Your baby is now the size of a haggis.

Rainbows are good for the baby.
Postmodernism is bad for the baby.
The baby enjoys what you enjoy
and that's absolutely fine,
unless what you enjoy is crack cocaine,
or eating too many nuts, or riding rollercoasters.
Use your common sense – oh,
the way you are sitting, right now, sweetie,
that is very bad for the baby.

Your baby is now the size of a small dog.

Pomegranate juice may taste like your grandmother
found it in the attic, but it has a connection
to the fertility myths of the ancient Greeks,
which is good for the baby. Whatever
is good for the planet is good for the baby.
At least that's something we can all agree on.
But what is good for you isn't always
good for the baby. Stop being so selfish.

Your baby is now the size of a fucking enormous turnip.

Remember what we said about pain.
And try not to worry. It's bad for the baby.

Contraction

When I said it felt like my hip bones were made of molten metal,
I knew you wished that I was an accountant
and had told you to "think of the most painful thing
ever and times it by a hundred" – maybe
it sounded overblown, pretentious,
but I was thinking of Wolverine,
stripped and strapped down,
blueprinted with the surgeon's felt tip;
how they broke him and mended him,
injecting his skeletal void with Adamantium;
how they monitored his vitals on a black screen
and watched the tank drain slowly while inside him
a metal tree eased out branches into limbs,
twigs into fingers and toes, stiffening
to tougher than anything; how, though he was healing
even as it happened, from that day on
anyone holding a magnet had him;
how easily his shining bones
would pop out through flesh, as if pulled from
well braised meat and fly into their hands;
how when they held that one small thing
it could make him weak, the thing that made him strong;
and I was thinking of how so soon, a stranger would be holding our son.

Sound Design

I say, we're going to need something more intense than this.
You say, we've already gone all out on pain –

there is nothing audible left.
I say, alright, let's just leave it hanging

for a few beats before we roll the tape.
There's something to be said for anticipation.

> *the weight of a finger held*
> *above the flat cassette-player's button*

Together we forge the silent cry
and it does the job better than we could have imagined,

so we seek out more grades of silence
to stretch our poor resources:

> *someone holding a telephone receiver,*
> *just holding it to their ear, just holding it*

> *the emptiness after a clean slap,*
> *the motionless 'o' of a sex-doll's mouth*

> *a heartbeat out of audible range,*
> *the dilation of a stranger's pupils*

We record them all, these things that should
announce themselves louder than lightning.

That last one, you say, we can use that
for fear, or for love.

After the Watershed. *Do I know Her?*

I am not so much afraid for her right now as I am afraid of her, though I could never admit it, never explain how the regularity of her pulse sets my teeth on edge – you learn too much about yourself – someone plugs my wife into a machine and it turns out public heartbeats bother me, there is

an embarrassing wetness to them. she is the machine – flesh and blood, but built for a purpose. she is a machine for pointing out her fecundity squeam piles on shock piles on horror piles on the desire to ignore everything that's happening and the power that she has over me, and life, and death.

I want to tell you she's a glorious meat-mech, she is more man than I am but her heart's wet kisses, their masculine insistence – putting everything into it – muscle, sinew, sweat, blood, shudder through my bones and balls – she is a machine for eviscerating gender. I'll admit I'm threatened by her

ability to be simultaneously hard and soft, she shines out of her own body like a light, embarrassingly bright and downright dangerous, threatening to short-circuit the hospital. what relief when her heart flips over itself like a fish in a bucket, when she breaks her uncanny rhythm and the nurse arrives

holding a hook to break her waters. and I feel a change as the timbre of her heartbeat shifts and her waters drench the floor – there is one less barrier between me and my baby and there is one more barrier between me and this wave generator I once called wife.

Before the Incision

Here comes a trickster with a cup,
and a feather to test my sense of humour.
I am not feeling ticklish. The plastic cup
holds iced-water up to its fourth thin rib.
The cold is pain, he tells me, asks:
Can you feel it now? How about now?

I don't suppose I can. At the edges of feeling
it is harder to perceive. My body is a boat
on my brain's horizon. Its hull, thick with pitch,
feels the ocean only as rubbery pressure,
then as the violent tug and haul of storm.
My green sail is raised and I brace for the squall.

How Large You Will Get

a guide for expectant humans

Largeness is all relative. Largeness is really a mental phenomenon. In comparison to spiders, even the big ones, you are all large. In comparison to the moon, not so much. The moon is your end point. You will begin the size that you are and to start with you will continue to be the size you are while your density increases imperceptibly. At this point you represent an excess of matter contained within the shape and size of your former self and, as such, become more than human. Standing next to counter-tops is unbearable for superhumans like you. When the largeness pressuring your lower abdomen outdoes the pressure for secrecy, you will become unnoticeably larger. You will become larger still. But not as large as you think you are, possibly larger than you would like or still not as large as you would like, dependent on company and frame of mind. At some point your largeness will elicit a smile from a fellow female commuter. Around the same time it will become necessary to use a hairband to secure your flies and at this point you are officially pregnant. You are now large enough to believe that everybody will notice your largeness, but you are not in actual fact that large until your largeness is ratified by the offer of a seat from a male commuter. Don't worry. You will soon be large enough to laugh at the tyranny of the flat stomach, to buy jeans with elasticated waists and to be offered seats. Enjoy it, because you will shortly pass into the public access zone, where your largeness is considered a suitable topic of conversation. Your favourite maternity top may become polished smooth or even worn through by the menagerie of strange hands that attempt to alight on your largeness unbidden. At this point you may be larger than you expected you would get and may discourage the taking of photographs. Remember at this stage that the moon is the end point. You are about to become larger than you thought possible and larger still. Shortly after eliciting your first outburst about "popping" from an elderly lady who is unknown to you, you may find you once again encourage the taking of photographs. Other humans may stare at you as if you have consumed your former self along with several passers-by, but you should feel free to remind them that largeness is all relative, that you are shooting for the moon here, and that there are things much larger even than the moon out there in the vacuum of space.

One Hell of a Show

They open me, cutting skin and tissue, draw muscles like curtains
and hold the folds with metal tie backs, to reveal the red front row.
And, good lord, this theatre is running all sorts of crazy productions.
There's the one where the woman under the knife laughs with the
                                        nurses even though
she can see her own blood spurting up onto the surgeon's gown,
the one where they stop to wash the dishes in her uterus mid-operation,
the one where everyone who talks to her is just a head and is upside-down.

> You are here! Suspended in the Super Troupers.
> We should shout, "Tah-dah!" at an entrance like this.
> For a second there is only you in your blurred halo,
> stamped on the moment's rosette, slick and bright.
> You are red, a baked bean, glistening in my juice.
> He announces you. You burst into sound and life.
> Tucked-up in the shape of my womb, haunches tight,
> you're a lion cub scruff-clamped, a tiny bloody Simba
> enraged at the circle of life, at the baboon
> who's holding you up, at your rude extraction.

> We are laughing because you are absolutely fine
> and all three of us are crying, because what else can you do?
> Everything fizzes, and while that may be the morphine,
> you are here. And I want you back now, I need you back.

When the curtains close, the show goes on regardless, only it's the one
where she wears the child for all time at her shoulder, where he blooms
like a fresh bullet hole, a mark that shows the villain where to stick his thumb,
the one where she is just an animal nursing her cub, nursing her wounds,
the one where they drop the surgical screen, and she cries out, "Oh!"
because her body lies knees splayed like a frog that's been run over,
though her brain still believes her legs are laid out straight before her.

ALIEN vs JONESY

INT. UNDERCARRIAGE ROOM - "C" LEVEL

Jones the cat enters.
Slinks between boxes.
Searching.
Chains clank.
The Alien shifts in the darkness.

                    ALIEN
          Treads another soft-shell - a nymph. Warm,
          mewing, incomplete. Wanting for the comfort
          of a host in which to moult, reform,
          become itself. Seeking chrysalis mother.

          Oh, saliva, acid-rush gullet.
          Lips, lips back, jaws all shudder
          and slaver - take your pleasure now, now -
          skull it!

Brett enters.
Still looking for Jones.
Another yowl followed by a hiss.
Two eyes shining in the dark.
Jones.
Relieved, Brett moves toward the cat.

                    JONESY
          Fssst - a snapped flare, from my x-ray
          bones to whiskers I am stiff objection.
          Cut from hard dark you are, bad spirit -
          of the humans, but not one of them. Tell me,
          what is so good about growing inside them?
          Why all the fuss over your inept exit?

          I have seen your kind before, though smaller,
          a bruised squall, pink lungbag, screaming
          into life, seen the tides of its entrance,
          through endless mopping, swallow the familiar
          ground. I know you have come to eviscerate
          our cosy routines. And you rise, hungry
          crucifix wanting a thief. Well, praise me!
          I have come armed with your stop-gap Jesus.

Brett reaches for Jones.
Jones hisses.

                    ALIEN
          Spit and keratin! All voltage, this menace –
          born cruel, the colour of poison carapace,
          snare-snap pupils, pin-mawed mug,
          concentrated disdain for blood.
          Let it live – grow into a host as delicious,
          as cruel. See – it bears a kind gift,
          true to its kind, it bears a cruel gift.

An arm reaches for Brett.

2nd, 3rd and 4th sets of screen directions taken from the shooting script for "ALIEN" by
Walter Hill and David Giler, based on the screenplay by Dan O'Bannon.

Lesson #1

You teach me that we are not born perfect.
We are not the adverts for human flawlessness
our own sayings would have us believe.

We are born with old men's hands,
with scalps like the hulls of ancient ships,
and yes, our fingernails may be perfect seashells,

but our toenails – gods! Our toenails
are the curled talons of changelings,
hardly aware at all that they are human things.

You are breathing without me

and this is as good as walking away.
Your peach-fuzz head cupped in my hand, your warmth, your squirm,
it all seems so present. But the evidence is there:
a stump on your belly, the mark of this first separation.

The future is here: all moments stacked upon one another,
cards in a deck that could be drawn in any order, at any moment –
you will hold your own head up and this is walking away,
you will feed yourself and this is walking away,
you will go to school and this is walking away,
you will sit up and this too is walking away,
you will say "mummy", but before you do you'll say "walk! walk!"
and "car" and "bird", and maybe "shoes".

And the first time you walk away towards a toy,
or the door, or someone else's open arms –
it has already happened, will always be happening,
because that will be now, and now is now,
and how could you do this to me, leaving,
before we've even got started?

I stare at you. You are so familiar,
as if you have always been here.
The thought folds beneath the weight
of all those future nows
and I get why they call them milestones - see it
unfurled and waymarked, the foreshortened road,
the distance between your helplessness and mine.

Please, before you leave, I need to fix this
moment, thread it through all other moments.

The only thing shielding us in this, this now,
is a stiff blue pleated curtain
made from a fabric found only in hospitals.
Let's pretend it's the edge of the world.

Born Free

Released back into the wild, she is uncertain. The instinct to feed is strong, but her infant is new to this. Patience is required. It is testament to the bond of motherhood that she perseveres. Many mammals faced at this early stage with such inept feeding might abandon their offspring. In this case, it seems to be a matter of the reward outweighing the pain and frustration of the initial struggle.

Dogged in his quest, her infant manages to get milk in his ear, in his left eye and on the far wall. A spot lands on the television screen, but is not fat enough to tumble over itself and run. She imagines herself rising to wipe it off, then turns her attention back to the business of establishing a good latch, to tickling this tiny stranger on the chin with her nipple, watching for the moment his mouth pops wide.

Plugged in, she nests in the long grass of the living room and watches endless documentaries about humans. Eventually, she picks up her book. One page in, she is faced with the problem of turning the page. She uses a combination of fingers, a knee and her infant's back to catapult the book to the middle of the rug where it stands erect on slightly fanned pages, inert, out of reach. She weeps, half-heartedly.

There is a noise in the long grass: footsteps. Someone enters. It is one of the humans from the documentaries, though this one is hunting neither for antiques, nor a husband, nor a killer. She holds her offspring close. The human bends with enviable ease, snaps up the startled book in one hand, returns it to her and takes her infant. She frisbees the book to the cushion beside her, holds her own hand. Waits apprehensively for her infant's safe return.

skin|skin

my skin gives the cue|your temperature aligns
with my every exhalation|you fall closer in to me
I am absorbing you|you are sinking
through my skin|you return to me
I am earth receiving|you are rainwater seeping
back into me|you settle

after your long adventures in the air

I stroke with my wrists|your back accepts
my most delicate offering|your little frog spine
so much is passed from me|to you in this way
my breath on your crown|your breath on my sternum
my pulse woomfing at your ear|your heart trundling on my ribcage
I give you my warmth|you surrender your weight

this is enough

skin|skin II

my sigh soul-rumble|your sigh valve-controlled
I contemplate myself in metal|you contemplate yourself in flesh
instructions delta brain to nerves|analysis, open, closed, response
muscle contracts|pistons engage
I raise my right hand|you raise your left hand

we touch

your cold sluices|my warmth is conducted
my fingerprint runnels|by your copper fingertips
pupils dilate|apertures adjust
stay my recoil|lock your position
I hold|you hold

we equalise

The Problem of the Tin Cans

The robot bodies are working. They are perfectly engineered.
The children can now hear and speak just like normal –
can hear better than the best of us –
have Creative Blaster Earache Supreme
ZX33 integrated sound cards.

What more can I do?

They can change the face that shows on their screen.
Can be girl, boy, black, white,
animal, anything they desire.
They have state-of-the-art robotic limbs,
could pinch a mote from a leveret's eye
with their patent-pending Soft-Touch fingertips,
catch Farah Junior on Duratech® legs.

What more can I give them?

The brain environment is optimal.
The feedback loops are fully functional.
The problem is not mathematical,
is not mechanical, is not my hardware
– how many times can I tell the boss that?
I run the diagnostics daily on each one,
plug them in, let it run overnight, every night.

But still they are fading.

Evaporating, dissolving, coming unstuck,
just stopping, just ceasing to exist. This morning,
I found another one. A shell,

absent as a coma patient, stalled in the corridor
halfway between the vending machine
and the maintenance lab. Just like the others,
its head was tilted, its metal arm outstretched,
little hand open, palm up,

as if asking for a screwdriver.

I'm in Costa with the other new mums again

and behind our eyes we are all as desperate not to talk about this as we are to talk about it. The looped security footage of our birth stories, with their statistics, their metaphors, and their "home-from-home" decor, masks what is really going on in our corridors, where we are slipping past galleried rooms in which they are taking scientists, artists, nurses, poets, marketing managers and teachers and cauterising their specialisms, where we are sneaking onto restricted levels through doors signed "Nulligravida Only" in an attempt to break into a party in the penthouse where well-groomed women in backless dresses are discussing and postulating and theorising and conceptualising and there is a balcony without a handrail from which you can see the infinite possibilities of the night sky…

Drink it In

That is the smell of new, the smell of freshly divided cells, scent bursting from the cruxes of their separations like spores from a puffball. Separation of body from body, the iron smell that follows the neat rasp of flesh sliced from flesh. That bold note is almost certainly blood.

It is the not so fresh but nonetheless compelling tang of meconium, the body's first tarry expulsion, seven days from its in utero shitting. It is the banana whiff of my colostrum, his first gold-topped tipple riding high along with particles of sick on his tufty mosaic of a scalp.

But most of all, I agree, the smell is sweet, a natural sweetness which, like honey, has the base undercurrent of excretion. This is the smell of vernix caseosa, the cheesy varnish that coats us all at birth, of nine months bathing in amniotic fluid – skin-drink, cushioning, gushing fanfare, that delicate suspension of nutrients, foetal urine and all the by-products of creation.

It's the smell of my uterus and I'm flattered you like it – no, don't be disgusted, be animal, be proud. There is a wild mother in you, and she needs to want to lick this heady cocktail from the newborn's eyes.

Happiness Not Included

The implant is small, but expensive,
words her father once used to describe her.
The promise is big and cheap –
Know her mind before she knows it herself!
Imagine her face! (she is opening a present)
Imagine her delight! (silhouettes entwine)
Imagine the perfect life together
where YOU need never be wrong again!
You take the special offer – who wouldn't?

       Down, into the algae-ridden
       pond of her mind, where her desires lurk
       like jewels in the midden.
       They loom out at you as jut-jawed pike,
       as flash-bulb minnow, or lie hidden
       glimmering in the depths amongst the murk
       and weeds, more precious for being forgotten.
       You'll know her now, with time, with luck.
       You tickle each want, lift it, slap it
       down on the slab of your need to know.
       Slit it open, finger-gut it
       and lay its entrails out just so.
       Do you see it? Can you pluck it
       from out the shit and blood and roe?

You feel them now even when you shouldn't,
can't switch it off. And yes, you have bought
a good gift or two, but your fingertips are flayed,
for there, amongst the things she'd never ask for,
lie pin-sharp bones: the things she'd never say.

I'm in Costa with the other new mums again

and behind our teeth we are all struggling with the existential crisis brought about by giving rise to another consciousness. The looped security footage of our birth stories, with their lifts, their malpractice, and their operating tables, masks what is really going on in our corridors, where we are hurrying past blue-curtained berths where mothers are losing their minds to empty mirrors and blank photographs, as if it were a trade, mind for mind, mother for child, one-for-one, where we are sneaking onto restricted levels, through doors signed "Priests and Philosophers Only" beyond which we are certain there's a rooftop pool where a mind can exist in brittle solitude and know itself and be known, and exist in and of itself, where you can float naked and alone in contemplation without even having to close your legs...

The Swarm

She is in the pub and all the words are bees, and the words she wants to hear are bees, spilling from the lips of her companions. They zip off unbidden into bee-thick air on bee-errands never to be seen again. She stares greedily as if the bees are humbugs, as if she can draw them in with her eyes. But the bees will not come to her empty hive. Now, a bee zips straight at her – HARROGATE – sunlit honeycomb. The Harrogate bee veers away at right-angles. She trails it, missing all the bees that follow – a single bee – a single bee is meaningless. Her friends laugh. And she laughs. Spills waves of her own dumb bees. Her guts thread through a cell at her core, the exact diameter of a bee. And her ears buzz and she can't hear, so how can she hear so many bees? All the mouths in the pub are wide as oak hollows. Each spills a column of bees and they swarm. And it is not a dream. And she weeps. And she weeps bees.

Glass, A Predicament

Isn't it bad luck, you ask,
to wear a dress of broken mirrors?
The seamstress is bullish

– *Nooooo!*
You are thinking of looking glasses.

You turn your head and the high collar
fingers up onto your cheeks,
splayed ice feathers, cut-throat razors,
testing the resolve of your skin.

You are thinking of dresses made of ladders!
she says. *Give us a twirl!*

You daren't. You can't.
You shift slightly and the fabric creaks,
smashed safety-glass, blanket of resistance,
a landscape of forced joints and grating folds.

You are thinking of dresses made of umbrellas
opened indoors!

Ought the ability to move not be prerequisite,
you say. How will I dance?
You lift an arm and the scraping
threads a cringe through your bones.

Forget dancing – can't you see yourself in this
walking down that aisle?

You stare in the achingly whole mirror,
imagine it – taking a step,
each tiny pane in the dress exploding,
sparkling the room in a galaxy of shards,
leaving you naked but for the backing gauze.
100% third act carnage.

I can see the whole world in it, you say,
and it is in pieces. Isn't it
bad luck? You ask again.

She says, *I don't know,*
are you the one who dropped the mirrors?

I'm in Costa with the other new mums again

and beneath our skin we are all itching with bodily awareness. The looped security footage of our birth stories, with their waters, their faeces, and their haemorrhaging, masks what is really going on in our corridors, where we are slipping past rooms with blacked out windows trying not to hear the screams or smell the freshly branded flesh, where we are sneaking onto restricted levels in an attempt to break ourselves out, through doors signed "Staff Please Ensure All Immunisations Are Up to Date", to the door behind which we are locked up and caged in and tied, gnawing at our shiny new bits, engraved with the words *I know what it is to be dead, I am meat, I am an animal in the wild right now; I know what it is to be animal, I am dead, in the wild I would be meat right now; I know what it is to be meat, I am an animal, in the wild I would be dead right now…*

The Snugness

She has kept all her old skins.
Sentimental, for a snake.

Each seemed outmoded when she sloughed it off,
but now – look at them! – parchment perfection.

Days like today, when she feels small,
she lays them out, sucks it all in

and eases her long way, nudging and nosing,
into the likeliest looking void.

Now, her breaths are whispered scraps –
this is never the good idea it seems.

Has anyone ever died like this? she wonders,
resting, just resting, half out, half in,

eaten whole by a past self,
suffocated by the tightness of their own skin.

circumscribed by those late crinolines, with their hoops of flattened steel, the red-black air beneath,

the ghosts of our children would spring back to shape with deadly efficiency hide and haunt us

our men believed no matter how small the carriage, how tight the door we could deliver

heirs and beautiful heirs, oh, cane and brass, both were well-beaten – no splintering genes please, no

miscarriages. no misshapen embarrassments upon standing no stain upon the jacquard

these cages were perfectly constructed to contain the stronger sex and all our secrets

in the precise shape required by the exacting whims of fashion of we all loved, but what woman

didn't weep when at the height of their width they extended six feet underground – our prisons

– large enough to engulf a good-sized gentleman – dragged in the bowels of the earth. All we had

up there was piss, shit, blood, grief, pleasure, but after the disappearance of an eminent

banker, crinolines began to be considered to be hiding more than potatoes and prolapses

sheer damnation irresponsible and dangerous – no wonder we needed all that space!

now Instagram shows we favour more sensible, more woman-centric ways of being hidden

and shown off – fuck fashion – these days we are free to wear what we like – yeah, you can say it

but try hiding all this in a pair of skinny jeans.

What He Makes of Me

Little pointillist – he latches on wrong and takes
my blood for his palette, my breast for his canvas
and I am too sleepy to quibble. When I wake

there is a cuticle of bruise above my nipple
where his top lip crept greedy and drew
the blood through my skin in purple prickles.

His mouth, popped open in milky reverie,
is dreaming of bright red flavours to come.
I press the bruise and wince. It delights:

a stiff shirt collar grazing a love bite;
uncertainty on a week-day morning.
I wonder how much he has had of me.

This ruthless creation machine is his own
study in red and white, pink as a valentine.
He would suck the blood right through my skin
to complete himself and I would let him.

Cute Aggression

We want to squeeze.
We want to squeeze tighter
and, yes, we want to bite.

He sees it in our eyes
and invokes his protector:
low grade disgust.

He poos frequently,
sheds skin, and stores
stale milk in his neck creases.

Prone on the change mat,
in real cute danger,
he urinates in my eye.

We laugh and pretend
it is funny, perfectly
natural. Cute, even.

But we squeeze
a little less tightly.
Stop biting.

Vibrations

Your first laugh escaped all ways,
not out through the mouth as I had expected.
You were only the length of my thighs.
Thighs I didn't know I could hear with.

A miniature squeezebox, your torso.
I placed one hand to its cassotto,
let the novice laugh, a chaos of notes,
wheeze up through palm to wrist to arm.

I kissed it, the laugh, right at your breastbone,
was eight again, playing my first harmonica,
feeling its sound on my buzz-shocked lips,
pure, unsullied by air, by earwax.

I laid you on my chest and felt the laugh
vibrate through skin and bone, to my heart
and the meat of my lungs and I understood,
suddenly, the mechanics of wireless charging.

It's the reason I stand closer to people
when they laugh. It's why I take off my shoes
to better get the joke. Why my hand twitches,
why my gaze falls to their shirt-buttons.

Yellow Bird

A conversation trapped in iPhone amber,
gives off more warmth than anything.

> *Yohyee. Yohyee birh.*
> Yes. A yellow bird.

The way you turn the cheap Easter gift
over and over like an artefact.

> *Yohyee.*
> Yes, yellow.
> *Yohyee birh.*
> Yes, yellow bird.

The way your eyes meet with mine
to greet comprehension, again and again.

Lung-song

Outside, the air is grating against itself,
the trees lift it in ovation, their cold applause

resounds amplified under the dome
the clouds have grown over us, a huge bruised

ribcage; the ceiling of our theatre.
An endless hunger of dark

clackering locusts are trapped up against it.
Your chest rises and, rasping, falls.

The Third Verse

I know I am a bad mother because **I have written you a song**
and the third verse makes you cry because it is about leaving home
which is something you never considered an option
and I think, well, I don't want to have to have this conversation
when he's forty or thirty or maybe even twenty,
and though **I named the song for you**, each time I sing it,
it pains me to miss out the offending verse
because it spoils the plot arc of the song,
if songs even have plot arcs,
and every time I near the end of **the second verse**
which **is something** anodyne **about night animals**
the last hovers on my lips like Judas' kiss

This is not the sort of rescue Hollywood has trained him for

They do not watch the news that morning, but
                everybody knows.
They go to the beach and have ice-cream
for breakfast.

And the beach is full
of people having ice-cream for breakfast
          in the shadow of the rockets.

He brings the giant chalks and they join
the ones who are cave-painting
on the walls of the city. Switch to felt pens
to make stained glass of the buildings
          their short lives

          we thought were the future.

And it is all tremendous fun.
And they do not watch the news that lunchtime.
They go home and get in the car
and he sits them in turn on his knee
          and they drive
          while he does the pedals.

They bake and build Lego and play all the games

and they both cheat
They eat

    and he lets them cheat.
when they want
and they eat what they want
    and the rockets are boarding

and when it gets dark they run outside
in their socks and stay up to watch the bats
and star-spot in the clutter of the night sky

They shh and beam and giggle.

because it's important
    to keep your promises.

It is way past bedtime.

And they do not watch the news that evening,
but he knows all the same
it is time to sleep,

the first bomb has dropped,
the rockets are leaving,
and it is time to sleep.

So he brings them hot chocolate,
tucks them up with kisses and lies
waiting.

Their bedtime drink makes them so dozy.

Their breathing settles.

He hugs the spare pillow to his chest

The bat looks bigger in tiny hands

It was your idea, but daddy put them in there. Just a single party packet of Haribo in a small rainbow donkey. But look at it now. Under the gaze of the circling children, it has grown to the size of a cart horse. *PIÑATA! PIÑATA!* – their cries strip the paint from the church hall walls and when their assault ruptures the belly it releases an endless fiesta of hell and sweetness. You regard the resulting carnage. Your scar itches.

Soft Play

I venture in because I think I hear crying,
and am met with a pregnant silence.
As I look back at where I entered
through a raw portal, a square blue scream,
at the metal frame padded and twined around,
bound like a warrior's calf, there's a click.

Instinct sends me diving to escape,
but it's too late: the steel gates drop.
The trap is sprung, all exits blocked.
The lights gutter and fail, give way
to an emergency glow the exact shade of red
you'd rather not see in an emergency.

When the snarling starts, I bolt, slip,
almost end in the caviar ball-pit.
Nylon netting kaleidoscopes my vision
as I struggle through diminishing tunnels,
a lobster in a creel – I'll be eaten alive –
and you two are in here somewhere, being small.
The rollers nearly take me – I lose a sock,
but have to desert it – screw the rules.
Where are you? Where the hell are you?
I call out your names and all noise stops.

Again there is silence. The silence of listening.
The beasts are turning their ears to me.

It starts again, club-loud, the air
pulsing with heartbeat, breathing, strain.
Claws skiffle round the corner behind me.
I close my eyes and duck. There's a yelp –

the sound of a beast taken down. I look,
catch a blur of sharp white yanked out of sight.
Your twin hollers echo on the corrugated walls
and repeat in the gullets of your tribespeople.
I am not the rescuer. I am not the one with training.
My kisses and inane songs are useless here.
I take off my other sock, clutch it like a weapon,
back into a corner and plant my bare feet
on the sticky matting. *Go on boys!* I call.
If nothing else, I can be the bait.

Yes, go on boys, let those hands go to work,
clambering, pulling my nightmares to pieces.
I know you are close. I can already hear
the ball-joints popping from their sockets.

WHAT YOU BRING WITH YOU

INT. GENERATION SHIP/MEDICAL BAY

CONCERNED MOTHER sits with her child.
Wrings her hands.
The SHIP'S DOCTOR snaps off his gloves.

                    CONCERNED MOTHER
          Tell me, Doctor – how bad is it?

                    SHIP'S DOCTOR
          I'm afraid it's space-lice.

                    CONCERNED MOTHER
          You promised us
          we were the future, promised us
          sights never sullied by man's gaze,
          a poet's paradise, you promised
          our descendants intrepid lives,
          lives straight from our comic-books.
          But – space-lice?

                    SHIP'S DOCTOR
          Space-lice, yes.

                    CONCERNED MOTHER
          Oh. But the adventure ends
          with us, doesn't it? This
          will be home to them, and the earth
          with its lush ferns and extensive elbow-room
          just a seldom-used setting on the holodeck.
          You promised us the heavens
          and you have delivered
          space-lice.

                    SHIP'S DOCTOR
          Well … they're just head-lice, really.
          But we are in space.

"A what?"

You point at an "oo" and say, "That's a digraph." And I know how religion feels in the face of science. How it feels to be needed completely, then to be needed not quite so much, then a little less still, until the day when a question comes and you are lost for an answer, or worse still, you are in the shoes of the asker. How it feels to have been the authority on everything, to have been always right in the eyes of the believer, to have been a balm for every ill. Mothers, we should keep something from them, leave a hole in their teachings to safeguard our godhead. Something we will pass on only if they become parents themselves and we are forced to surrender the names they called us. But the only thing we can keep from them that long is how much we have loved them, and they us, and they will never believe that they don't already know it until the day that they do. By the time all this has passed through my head, I think I understand what the word means, but the question has already filled my open mouth and I am kneeling, and you are holding the book, so I ask it anyway.

The Truth Machine

He stands like a little tin soldier in the front drive.
Why hasn't this been done before?
The lack of opportunity, I suppose,
between the coming of language and the departure of innocence.
I plug in the neon sign at his side and give it a dunt.
Its colours pop, an unnatural bloom.

From him, every reaction, every emotion, is truth.
For his smiles, he demands nothing.
There is no agenda, there are no preconceptions.
There is just the thing and the observer and the truth of it.
Primary colours, his emotions.
A spade is a spade, but oh my word – a spade!
Do you see how it digs? Think of the holes we could make!
Look at the shining line along its back
that moves when I move the spade – how does it do that?
A spade is all possibility and all beauty
and everything is a spade.

I can see the queues all the way from here to Slough.
Those who have never seen the truth.
Those who have had it and lost it.
Those who want to see the world anew, without its orbital debris
of tit and tat.

"Let's check he's working," says my Mum.
She pops 20p in the coin slot, kneels,
smiles and waits. He studies her face,
eyes tracing with care the journey of each wrinkle.
His neon sign flickers, then he speaks.

Unwritten Messages

You say, if you were lost at sea
you would send a message in a bottle
to get help.

My little sailor, I say, if you were lost at sea
you might not have a bottle.
You might not have paper.
You might have paper and a bottle,
but nothing to write with.
Or all three and no solid surface to lean on.

Your eyes widen
and begin to shine. Silent, distant,
like tears shed elsewhere.

Son, just call me Penfold, because

crumbs, DM! Where are they coming from?
Cascading from your sleeves as you go,
raining from your face as if your chin
is that dinky drawer beneath the toaster –
no, don't open your mouth – don't move –
let me hoover you, borrow a dog
from somewhere, roll you up like a rug
and shake you out of the window. Crumbs!
Sometimes I fear they are coming from you,
that you are crumbling away inside
your clothes, that one day all that will be left
will be a trail of crumbs through the house,
a hollow school uniform in a heap on the rug,
that I will poke it tentatively with my toe
and it will crunch like a loosely-packed sack
of sweepings from the Paxo factory floor.

JUDGEMENT DAY

EXT. COMPOUND - DAY (LATE AFTERNOON)

SARAH'S HEAD droops. She closes her eyes.

                    SARAH
          This could be the playground from my
          nightmares.

The grass is EXIT green
And the sun is shining.

          The young mothers' patience is endless,
          they are fairy lights, rubber ducks –

          they still know how to be fun,
          know how to play with their kids.

          And she is always there, taking his hands,
          making safe his bid to master balance.

This waitress in candyfloss nylon,
she turns to us, laughing.

          No! I shout - my words are empty shapes.
          No! You need to run! I know what's coming.

          She turns away as if I am a shadow
          cast upon the fence, a trick of the light.

          I slap my palms against the chicken wire
          and rail against everything that makes her me.

THE SKY EXPLODES. The children
ignite like match heads.

          I grip the fence-links, reel and scream
          and burn. As if we could outrun this.

          Sarah is burning, overexposed,
          shields our burning boy, screaming.

          And that is when it hits me, every time:
          I am the nightmare. I am the blast.

The shockwave moves through them,
blasting them to ash and Sarah...

          This is just one of many endings.

Wakes up.

Left-aligned screen directions and isolated phrases taken/adapted from "TERMINATOR 2: JUDGMENT DAY", a screenplay by James Cameron and William Wisher (revised final shooting script).

In Defence of Never Blinking

No, not even sequencing can tell you
where a child's eyes will come to rest:
blue, or brown, or, hope-against-hope,
most sought-after green.

Even after all these years, in certain lights,
you think, after all, perhaps they have not yet
settled, that they will keep on changing.

That one day your child will regard you
and their irises will be pitch, or plum, or crimson,
and you will not know when it happened,
and it will be too late, now, to mention it.

The Holodeck

The floor moves with me as I walk. I can never outrun it. I conceived this earth-walk as a grand escape. Planned my route as if winding yarn about the world. Won't miss an inch. It started well, with forests of synthetic green, deer leaping invisible hurdles, more – cities, deserts, ice. A month in, my daughter joins me. But by now I am walking the ocean floor and have been for weeks. We walk in silence. See nothing but a slow-moving spider-crab, the picked-clean bone hull of a whale. *Is this what it's like?* she asks. *Earth, is this why you left?* She tries to catch my eye. *Mostly*, I say and take her hand. The floor moves with us as we walk.

Some ways to love them

When the foxes bark, linger long at the light switch.
Walking, seek fervently that perfect fit of hand in hand.

At any o'clock, drop your hat and chase the wishie seeds
they've foofed from their dandelion to see where they will land.

When they bring their sleep to you, hesitate to lay them down,
hold their sleeping self like a Dior gown in your arms.

At the fever's call, bring them home to your skin again.
Though each kiss evaporates, still brand them with its charm.

Insatiable swat, map their body, watch each quirk,
learn their whole by heart with a scholar's intent.

Every morning, see them as if they are new again,
be awestruck at their fingernails, be desperate for their scent.

With them, with each other, play headlong, with abandon,
in thanks for the gift. Grasp the joy, every sliver.

Even in your anger, love with purpose, with the need
of salmon swimming home against the run of the river.

Hello, guts!

I knew there might be the odd nipple-shot
when I agreed to show you the photos of his birth.

But I hadn't noticed that yellow-swabbed rectangle
around what I want to call the exit wound.

Didn't realise that these pictures could afford you
the opportunity to see quite so far inside of me.

Acknowledgements

Poems from this collection have appeared in *From Glasgow to Saturn*, *The Interpreter's House*, *Magma*, *Mslexia*, *The North Magazine*, *The Poetry Review*, *Shoreline of Infinity*, and *Wales Arts Review*. "ALIEN vs JONESY" first appeared in the Sidekick Books anthology *Lives Beyond Us: Poems and Essays on the Film Reality of Animals.* "Some Ways to Love Them" was commended in the Troubadour International Poetry Prize 2019. "Contraction", "This is Not the Sort of Rescue Hollywood Has Trained Him For" and "Unwritten Messages" were translated into Greek for the Vakxikon Publications *Anthology of Young Scottish Poets*.

I'd like to say thanks to Kate Potts, Holly Hopkins, Alison Winch, Kim Moore, Jon Stone and John McCulloch for their invaluable feedback on a number of these poems, to my husband Matthew for his continued support and input, and to the late Roddy Lumsden for reassuring a heavily-pregnant me that children wouldn't put a stop to my poetry.

EXT. BROKEN SLEEP BOOKS - LAY OUT YOUR UNREST